Practice in the Basic Skills

KT-176-804

Contents

Published by Collins Educational
An imprint of HarperCollins*Publishers* Ltd
77-85 Fulham Palace Road
London W6 8JB

www.CollinsEducation.com
On-line support for schools and colleges

© Derek Newton and David Smith 2003
First published 1978
This edition published 2003
Reprinted 10 9 8 7 6 5 4 3 2 1

ISBN 0 00 717714 3

The authors assert the moral right to be identified as the authors of this work.

All rights reserved. No part of this publication may be reproduced, stored in a retrieval system, or transmitted in any form or by any means, electronic, mechanical, photocopying, recording or otherwise, without either the prior permission of the Publisher or a licence permitting restricted copying in the United Kingdom issued by the Copyright Licensing Agency Ltd, 90 Tottenham

Court Road, London W1P 0LP. This book is sold subject to the condition that it shall not by way of trade or otherwise be lent, hired out or otherwise circulated without the Publisher's prior consent.

British Library Cataloguing in Publication Data
A catalogue record for this book is available from the British Library.

Illustrated by A Rodger

Printed by Martins the Printers Ltd, Berwick-upon-Tweed

Picture vocabulary

Write the names of these **mammals**.
Write a short description of any *five* of them.

Pronouns

A Write out the **pronouns** in the following sentences.

 1 Clive thinks he is the best swimmer in the school. .
 2 We caught the boys and they admitted stealing the apples.
 3 He saw me and he returned the book.
 4 I thanked her and she gave it to me.
 5 Please pass them to me.
 6 She asked whether they would be able to go with her.
 7 When you have read this book please pass it on to him.
 8 They told him that they would meet us at 10 o'clock.
 9 She said that it belonged to her.
10 He was given 50p but he lost it.

B Use a **pronoun** to *show possession* instead of the words in the brackets.

 1 This ball is (belongs to my sister).
 2 This bicycle is (belongs to me).
 3 This rabbit is (belongs to my sister and me).
 4 This cricket bat is (belongs to my brother).
 5 This wheelbarrow is (belongs to my neighbours).
 6 This tennis racket is (belongs to you).

C Complete these sentences by adding the correct **pronoun**.

 1 The girls hurried so that _____ would not miss the train.
 2 Alan's mother asked _____ to cut the grass.
 3 The dog buried a bone and could not find _____ .
 4 As my friend and I walked towards the river, a policeman stopped
    _____ .
 5 Will _____ please tell Mrs. Clark that Sandra will collect _____
    shopping?

Alphabetical order

A Write the names of these objects in **alphabetical order**.
Look at the *second* letter.

1

Do the same with these words.

2 pull   pity   pygmy   pan   polish   plum
3 hymn   help   hobby   hawk   high   huge
4 fear   foot   funny   field   fair   flat
5 witch   wrote   whirl   worm   wash   week

B Write the names of these objects in **alphabetical order**. Look at the *third* letter.

1

Do the same with these words.

2 bay   bath   banana   basket   baboon   barley
3 fan   fail   fast   family   factory   fall
4 ham   hatch   hair   hawk   harp   habit
5 meat   merge   message   mend   mellow   meet

C Write these in **alphabetical order**, looking at the *fourth* letter.

1 forward   forfeit   fork   forbid   form   forget
2 paternal   path   patter   patch   patrol   patience
3 canvas   cane   canyon   candid   cancel   canoe
4 manly   mankind   mansion   manager   mane   manor

Picture vocabulary

Write the names of these **means of transport**.
Write a short description of any *five* of them.

Vocabulary—associations

A What do you associate with each of the following?

1 an aquarium	**5** a hangar	**9** a reservoir
2 barracks	**6** an aviary	**10** a refinery
3 a museum	**7** an orchard	**11** a hold
4 a silo	**8** a studio	**12** a vineyard

B Place these people in the positions of authority each holds.

> keeper   editor   director   president   conductor
> headteacher   matron   captain   judge   sister
> governor   principal

1 _____ of a school

2 _____ of a hospital ward

3 _____ of a ship

4 _____ of a college

5 _____ of animals in a zoo

6 _____ of a firm or company

7 _____ of a prison

8 _____ of a republic

9 _____ of a newspaper

10 _____ of a hospital

11 _____ of a court of law

12 _____ of an orchestra

C What special names are given to books which contain

1 the meanings of words?

2 the story of a person's life?

3 a collection of maps?

4 a record of daily happenings?

5 a collection of poems?

6 a detailed, daily record of a ship's progress?

7 pictures, newspaper cuttings, etc?

8 facts about many kinds of knowledge?

9 telephone numbers?

10 a collection of postage stamps?

Verbs—sounds

A Choose **verbs** which convey a *sound* to complete these sentences.

1 Steam _____ from the damaged radiator.
2 The car wheels _____ on the loose stones.
3 At dawn, in the forest, the birds _____ happily.
4 During the storm hailstones _____ against the windows.
5 The glass _____ when the cricket ball hit the window.
6 The rusty hinges on the castle door _____ loudly.

B Complete the following by using *sound* words.

1 The _____ of water.
2 The _____ of an explosion.
3 The _____ of leaves.
4 The _____ of a rifle.

5 The _____ of a bell.
6 The _____ of paper.
7 The _____ of hoofs.
8 The _____ of donkeys.

C Complete these.

1 The boom of a _____ .
2 The howling of _____ .
3 The slam of a _____ .
4 The clanking of _____ .

5 The hoot of an _____ .
6 The shuffle of _____ .
7 The wail of a _____ .
8 The throb of an _____ .

D Complete these by adding a sentence which shows the *cause* of the sound.

1 Splash!

2 Whoosh!

3 Rat-tat-tat!

4 Bang! Crash!

Spelling

These words have either **ei** or **ie** missing. Write them out correctly.

1 w __ __ ght   5 misch __ __ f   9 for __ __ gn   13 s __ __ ze

2 n __ __ ce   6 dec __ __ ve   10 r __ __ ndeer   14 cash __ __ r

3 n __ __ ghbour   7 retr __ __ ve   11 anc __ __ nt   15 conc __ __ t

4 shr __ __ k   8 c __ __ ling   12 rec __ __ pt   16 ch __ __ f

Vocabulary

Rewrite these sentences replacing the words in bold type with words of your own.

1 After the long walk Jayne slept **like a log**.
2 I shouldn't like to be **in your shoes**!
3 It's **touch and go** whether the dam bursts.
4 Old Mrs. Baxter is finding it difficult to **make both ends meet**.
5 It rained **cats and dogs** most of our holiday.
6 I'm always **hard up** before the end of the week.

Punctuation

Write out the following sentences putting in all the necessary **commas, full stops** and **capital letters**.

1 clive paul and craig play golf every saturday and sunday
2 mrs marsden told janet to take the cakes to aunty margaret
3 in our easter holidays we went to london and saw buckingham palace and the bank of england
4 his friends who were becoming anxious telephoned leeds police station a policeman soon arrived
5 trevor francis became the first one million pound footballer when he was transferred from birmingham city to nottingham forest
6 for sunday lunch bob and roger had pork chops cabbage carrots and roast potatoes

Abbreviations

What do the following **abbreviations** stand for?

1 NSPCC	**5** Co.	**9** RNIB	**13** BST
2 RAC	**6** BR	**10** WWF	**14** UK
3 USA	**7** MCC	**11** IMF	**15** AFC
4 RNLI	**8** YOC	**12** NATO	**16** GM

Opposites

Write the **opposites** of these words.

1 depart _____	**5** rapid _____	**9** majority _____
2 seldom _____	**6** minimum _____	**10** moving _____
3 wealth _____	**7** barren _____	**11** legal _____
4 guilty _____	**8** retreat _____	**12** internal _____

Synonyms

Write words which are **similar in meaning** to these.

1 commence _____	**5** gigantic _____	**9** permit _____
2 expensive _____	**6** horizontal _____	**10** abandon _____
3 exterior _____	**7** ferocious _____	**11** duplicate _____
4 remedy _____	**8** insolent _____	**12** transparent _____

Homonyms

For each of the following words write another word which **sounds exactly the same** but is spelt differently.

1 sore _____	**5** root _____	**9** isle _____
2 medal _____	**6** wait _____	**10** principle _____
3 key _____	**7** bridle _____	**11** doe _____
4 rap _____	**8** pedal _____	**12** ceiling _____

Adjectives

A Choose a suitable **adjective** to complete the following phrases.

e.g. a <u>steep</u> hill

1 a _____ book
2 a _____ motor car
3 the _____ cliffs
4 a _____ party
5 the _____ river

6 a _____ winter
7 some _____ trees
8 a _____ holiday
9 the _____ mountaineer
10 a _____ storm

B These lines of words are all adjectives. Write out the adjective which has the **strongest** meaning.

e.g. fierce, wild, <u>brutal</u>, cruel, unfair

1 large, huge, big, gigantic, sizeable
2 shiny, clear, brilliant, bright, glowing
3 attractive, lovely, nice, pretty, beautiful
4 sad, unhappy, discouraged, miserable, dejected
5 cool, chilly, nippy, icy, wintry
6 tall, high, lofty, towering, elevated

C Rewrite the following phrases, choosing an **opposite** to the adjective in each phrase.

1 a patient driver
2 a harmful sting
3 a rude boy
4 the interior walls
5 a blunt knife
6 the alert guard dog

7 an ordinary holiday
8 a temporary building
9 the maximum score
10 the optimistic girl
11 a counterfeit bank note
12 the opaque glass

Spelling and vocabulary

A All these answers begin with **s** and have something to do with the sea.

1 a plant which grows in the sea   s _ _ _ _ _ _
2 a lot of fish swimming together   s _ _ _ _ _
3 an underwater ship   s _ _ _ _ _ _ _ _
4 a large fish with rows of sharp teeth   s _ _ _ _ _
5 a swimmer using flippers and a mask   s _ _ _ _   _ _ _ _ _ _

B All these answers begin with **ex**.

1 Plenty of _____ is good for your health.
2 Dr. Livingstone _____ parts of the African continent.
3 The runways were _____ so that Jumbo jets could land.
4 The dentist _____ two of my teeth.
5 You can't expect me to buy that bicycle, it's too _____ .

C Write the **group name** for each of the following collections.

1 lemon, peach, plum, lime, apple, orange
2 onion, lettuce, cabbage, leek, turnip, bean
3 square, hexagon, triangle, rectangle, octagon
4 lead, zinc, aluminium, gold, platinum
5 Arctic, Pacific, Atlantic, Indian, Antarctic

D Add two words which belong to each of these **groups** of words.

1 crocus, narcissus, hyacinth, snowdrop
2 golf, squash, tennis, rounders
3 Venus, Earth, Mars, Pluto
4 Sandra, Susan, Stella, Sarah
5 eagle, vulture, owl, hawk

Vocabulary

A All these are worn on the head.
What are they? Who would wear them?

B Write the word which names each of these groups.

   1 rye, barley, oats, wheat, maize
   2 BBC, YHA, JP, BSc, PTO
   3 pike, roach, perch, carp, tench
   4 Smith, Aitken, Hughes, Perkins, O'Hara
   5 hamster, beaver, rabbit, mouse, squirrel
   6 grasshopper, fly, butterfly, wasp, ladybird
   7 parsley, bay, thyme, sage, rosemary
   8 mahogany, teak, oak, walnut, beech

C What is the name of

   1 a room where typists and clerks work?
   2 the room where meals are cooked on board a ship?
   3 a room where a photographer develops films?
   4 the room in a bank where money and valuables are kept?
   5 a small room used for sleeping on board a ship?
   6 a room where prisoners are kept in prison?

Indirect speech

Change these sentences to **indirect speech**.

1 "My football boots need new laces," said Danny.
2 The policeman said to my dad, "You aren't allowed to park your car in this street."
3 "Has the train to Walsall gone?" asked Heather.
4 Aunty Shirley said to me, "I hope you like your birthday present."
5 I said to the librarian, "Have you a copy of 'Oliver Twist'?"
6 Marian said, "I go swimming twice a week."
7 "I am afraid, Brian," snapped Mr. Rigby, "that you are not working hard enough to pass the exam."
8 "Norma," asked the teacher, "will you bring the tape recorder, please?"
9 "Come on, slow coach," shouted George. "We'll miss the bus if we don't hurry."
10 "I'm sorry, George, but I'm running as fast as I can," panted Mildred.

Present and past tense

Copy and complete this table.

present tense	past tense	present tense	past tense
1 give		11	threw
2 know		12	forgot
3 catch		13	built
4 feel		14	rang
5 leave		15	stole
6 swim		16	brought
7 strike		17	held
8 lie		18	shook
9 begin		19	drove
10 drink		20	flew

Direct speech

Change these sentences to **direct speech**.

1 Simon asked me how tall I was.
2 My mother wanted to know if I was ready for tea.
3 Elizabeth shouted to Susan to be quick.
4 The mechanic told Mr. Barnes that his car would be ready on Tuesday.
5 Pat's mother asked her if she had finished her homework.
6 Paul told his dad that he had been chosen to play for the school cricket team.
7 Derek asked Mark whether he wanted to go fishing with him.
8 Mrs. Bladen told her son, Andrew, that he must not miss the last bus home.
9 Harry Cox shouted that he was trapped on his roof.
10 Mr. Green asked David to clean the windows and brush the floor.

Incorrect sentences

Rewrite these sentences correctly.

1 The dog and the cat was lying on the carpet.
2 Malcolm learned me to play badminton.
3 Was it her or him which spoke to you?
4 Dawn could not see her dog nowhere.
5 You can lend my bicycle if you're careful.
6 Patrick catched too perch in the canal.
7 The reward was divided between the three boy's.
8 Have you spoke to your father?
9 My brother is taller than me.
10 Neither the boys nor the girls has finished there work.

Picture story

Look carefully at the six pictures.
Write a story, in six paragraphs, that is interesting, exciting and has a humorous ending.

Contractions

Write out these **contractions** in full.

1 mustn't	**6** who'd	**11** won't
2 that's	**7** where's	**12** they'll
3 I'll	**8** wouldn't	**13** there'd
4 we've	**9** she'll	**14** it's
5 you're	**10** they've	**15** we'll

Vocabulary

Choose the correct word from the brackets to complete these sentences.

1 Linda _____ her homework as soon as she came home.   (done, did)

2 Bill and Danny _____ an exciting film last night.   (saw, seen)

3 Do you know _____ is coming to see us?   (who, whom)

4 You and _____ will have to cut the old lady's lawn.   (me, I)

5 Did you borrow _____ books from the library?   (them, those)

6 Will you _____ me to play squash?   (teach, learn)

7 The farmer wondered _____ his cattle _____ .   (were, where)

8 Have you _____ Freda? Yes, I _____ her getting on a bus.
(saw, seen)

9 The football captain wants to see you and _____ .   (me, I)

10 It's _____ late _____ go out with your _____ friends.
(to, two, too)

Adjectives

Use the correct form of the **adjective** in the brackets to complete these
sentences.

1 Spain is a _____ country than Britain.   (warm)

2 Jonathan did _____ work than Wayne.   (little)

3 Sarah is the _____ _____ member of our class.   (honest)

4 Bob is the _____ of the two brothers.   (clever)

5 Of all the rooms in our house this is the _____ .   (cosy)

6 Mrs. Arnold is _____ _____ than her sister.   (generous)

Plurals

Rewrite these sentences in the **plural** form.

1 Yesterday the workman repaired the roof.
2 I saw a calf, a horse, a goose and a donkey on the farm.
3 The policewoman caught the thief in the act.
4 The old lady twisted her ankle on the stony beach.
5 The boy fell off the rock and hurt himself.
6 My cousin came to see me last weekend.
7 The girl's pencil was in that box.
8 The school play wasn't very well acted.
9 The postman delivered a letter and a parcel to the house in the valley.
10 I do not think you understand the problem.

Spelling

There is **one spelling mistake** in each of these sentences. Find it and write the word correctly.

1 We all laughed at the puppy's behavior.
2 Janet was very tearfull when she fell off her bicycle.
3 I saw the rabbit dissappear down that hole.
4 Neither John nor Betty has compleated the work.
5 The policeman siezed the frightened dog.
6 Allthough he was near exhaustion, Bill finished the race.
7 Heather replied sensably to the teacher's questions.
8 There was a beatiful display of roses in the entrance hall.
9 In warm weather Gaynor allways wears sandals.
10 Mum knitted a woolen jersey.

Vocabulary—verb association

A Pair each **verb** in column A with its correct meaning from column B.

A	**B**
1 to conceal	scoop out; uncover by digging
2 to demolish	search into; examine closely
3 to substitute	put an end to; stop by force
4 to suppress	burst forth
5 to excavate	hide
6 to investigate	make pure
7 to erupt	pull or tear down; destroy
8 to refine	replace one thing or person with another

B Complete these sentences by choosing the most suitable verb formed from those in column A above.

1 The troops _____ the rebellion by firing on the mob.
2 Lava and ashes _____ from the volcano.
3 The archaeologists _____ part of an ancient buried city.
4 Sugar, oil and metals are _____ before being used.
5 Our goalkeeper, Colin, was injured and Alec was _____ .

C Of which **animal** does the person speaking remind you, in each of these sentences?

1 "My throat is very sore. I can hardly swallow," **croaked** Graham.
2 Mr. Ash **bellowed**, "Keep off my grass or I'll get the police."
3 The fans **screamed** with delight when their favourite pop group appeared.
4 My uncle Jim **droned** on and on about his family's history.
5 The huge crowd **roared** when the leader of the marathon entered the stadium.

Spelling and vocabulary

A Who are the following people? All the answers end in **ist**.

1 someone who plays a piano
2 a person who uses a typewriter
3 someone who knows about science
4 a person who writes novels
5 someone who drops from an aircraft by parachute
6 a person who makes a doll appear to speak
7 someone who sings songs alone
8 a person who looks on the bright side of things

B The answers to these clues all begin with **att**.

1 a room in the roof of a house
2 to try to do something
3 to start a fight
4 pleasing to look at
5 to fasten; to join

C The answers to these clues all end with **ture**.

1 a hole made with something pointed
2 the measure of how hot or cold something is
3 to take a prisoner
4 articles needed in a home e.g. chairs, beds
5 to cause very much pain

D The answers to these clues have **rr** in them.

1 to disagree; to argue angrily
2 a looking glass
3 to give in
4 a small dog
5 a place where stone is obtained from the ground

Analogies

Complete these **analogies**.

1 Kennel is to dog as _____ is to horse.
2 _____ is to rabbit as wool is to sheep.
3 Elephant is to _____ as pig is to grunts.
4 Gander is to goose as ram is to _____.
5 Hind is to fawn as _____ is to leveret.
6 Beaver is to lodge as badger is to _____ .
7 Snake is to _____ as frog is to croaks.
8 _____ is to scales as bird is to feathers.

Verbs

Rewrite the following sentences by choosing a **verb** which means the same as the words in bold type.

1 Don't tease that guard dog or it may **go for** you.
2 Karen is **going through** a lot of pain because of her broken tooth.
3 Stephen **goes in for** every chess tournament in the district.
4 Dogs often **go after** cats.
5 The council are determined to **go through with** their plan to build a new bridge.
6 Shops have sales when prices of goods **go down**.

Vocabulary

Use *one word* to express each of the following.

1 cheering and clapping
2 the highest point
3 someone who watches a game
4 a very great shortage of food
5 a slow-moving river of ice
6 someone who hoards money

Pronouns

A Complete these sentences by choosing one of the **pronouns** from this list.

yourselves	himself	myself	yourself	herself

1 "Are you sure you wrote this story _____ , Joan?"
2 "I can manage to lift it _____ , thank you."
3 "All right, you and Bob may stay, but you must make _____ useful."
4 Jayne enjoyed _____ at the party.
5 Tom fell awkwardly and hurt _____ .

B Each of these sentences contains one **pronoun**. Write it down and the **noun(s)** it replaces.

1 "You may come out now," Mrs. Morris said to Steven.
2 The hurricane had stopped but it caused a lot of damage.
3 Paul and Sally worked on until they had finished painting the kitchen.
4 Jacqueline asked Beryl to lend her 50p.
5 "Listen to me, children," said Mr. Morris.

C Write the correct **pronoun** in singular or plural form.

singular	plural		singular	plural
1 I		6		ours
2 myself		7		us
3 it		8		their
4 hers		9		yourselves
5 me		10		themselves

Contractions

Write these sentences using a **contraction** in place of the words in bold type.

1 **Where have** you been since tea?
2 Brian **does not** play rugby anymore.
3 **You would** be better if you practised more.
4 My dog **will not** obey me.
5 You **cannot** get in the concert without a ticket.
6 I **do not** know where Patrick has gone.
7 **I would** be very pleased if **you would** work harder.
8 I **shall not** be able to go fishing tomorrow.
9 **I will** see if **they are** ready to start.
10 **They have** had their chance so **it is** up to you to take yours.

Incorrect sentences

Write these sentences correctly.

1 My brother learned me how to ride a bike.
2 Joan acted good in the play.
3 Seamus wouldn't give me none of his toffees.
4 There is a lot of mountains in Austria.
5 Terry ran home as quick as he could.
6 A man and his dog was waiting outside the shop.
7 Beryl could not come no quicker.
8 Your fishing rod is different to mine.
9 The best team won the game.
10 The group sung the same song twice.
11 Poor Lesley couldn't remember nothing.
12 Between you and I, I don't think he is the right choice for captain.

Vocabulary

Write out the one word in each line which stands for all the other words.

1 sympathy   love   pity   anger   rage   feeling   hate
2 jumping   skating   running   exercising   swimming   walking
3 sapphire   ruby   gem   opal   diamond   emerald
4 flat   house   dwelling   bungalow   maisonette   apartment
5 tomorrow   time   afternoon   evening   today   yesterday

Jumbled letters

Here are six pictures of birds. Name them by rearranging the groups of letters—they are not below the correct pictures.

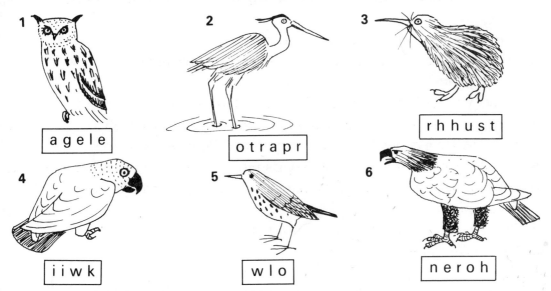

1   a g e l e

2   o t r a p r

3   r h h u s t

4   i i w k

5   w l o

6   n e r o h

Associations

Write the following words in pairs that go together.

set A		set B	
1 photographer	whistle	1 actress	laboratory
2 jockey	baton	2 keeper	kitchen
3 referee	spanner	3 chemist	office
4 doctor	camera	4 astronomer	studio
5 conductor	brush	5 typist	theatre
6 mechanic	saddle	6 chef	observatory
7 decorator	stethoscope	7 artist	lighthouse

Adverbs

A Write out the **adverbs** in these sentences.

1 Peter plays golf regularly.

2 Sandra looked dejectedly at her damaged bicycle and started to cry loudly.

3 I am coming now but I must go soon.

4 "The circus is held twice daily," shouted Tom excitedly.

5 "Put it there!" Ian ordered angrily.

6 "Have you looked everywhere?" asked Barry sadly.

7 "I cannot find your puppy anywhere," answered Janet sadly.

8 Tom has always been a good batsman and he bowls well too.

9 All the deer ran away into the woods when they heard us shouting loudly.

10 I once saw a fisherman catch a huge salmon which struggled frantically to escape.

11 "We have never met before," replied Harriet.

12 They have to run twice round the park.

B Choose suitable **adverbs** to complete the following.

1 The teacher explained _____ .

2 Our team lost _____ .

3 Mark answered _____ .

4 I remember _____ .

5 We visit Cardiff _____ .

6 The injured men staggered _____ .

7 The baby chuckled _____ .

8 She spoke _____ .

9 The rude boy sneered _____ .

10 The cyclist was injured _____ .

11 Shirley listened _____ .

12 They arrived _____ .

13 Our team won _____ .

14 The lost dog wandered _____ .

15 The hungry boy ate his food _____ .

16 The two ladies waited _____ .

Opposites

Rewrite these sentences, changing *one word* in each sentence to give the **opposite** meaning.

Do not use <u>was not</u> or <u>wasn't</u>, etc.

1 Alan's invention was a failure.
2 The yacht sailed through the rough seas.
3 Sarah checked the time as she left the office.
4 It was possible for the mountain to be climbed.
5 Bobby admitted that he had left the tap running.
6 The passengers were very patient when the plane was delayed.
7 Our teacher was discouraged by our exam results.
8 About one third of Jayne's answers were correct.
9 The majority of our class come to school by bus.
10 Tom helped his dad to push the car forwards.

Vocabulary

Rewrite the following sentences by choosing *one word* instead of those in bold type.

1 We managed to **put out** the fire.
2 Workmen have **put up** a bus shelter in our street.
3 You can do it! Don't be **put off** by their failure.
4 You will have to **put by** some money for your holidays.
5 The old lady couldn't **put up with** the loud noise of the machines any longer.
6 After losing a sail in a violent storm, the yacht **put into** port for repairs.
7 Sally was **put out** by the way her friends behaved towards her.
8 The football match was **put off** because of the frozen ground.

Verbs

These fifteen verbs end in **ate**.

celebrate	rotate	hesitate	meditate	elevate
lubricate	emigrate	narrate	associate	relate
cultivate	educate	germinate	imitate	dilate

The meanings of *ten* of these verbs now follow. Match these meanings correctly with the verbs.

1 to oil or grease machinery
2 to tell the story of
3 to think quietly
4 to prepare and use soil for crops
5 to make or become larger or wider

6 to do the same as someone else
7 to turn like a wheel
8 to help people to learn; to teach
9 to tell; give an account of
10 to leave own country
     and settle in another

Completing sentences

In each of the following sentences there are two dashes. Choose suitable words from this list to complete the sentences.

so, that	such, that	neither, nor	whether, or	if, then	either, or

1 ＿＿＿＿＿＿ my sister ＿＿＿＿＿＿ my brother has had chicken pox.
2 I am fishing this afternoon, ＿＿＿＿＿＿ you come with me ＿＿＿＿＿＿ not.
3 ＿＿＿＿＿＿ you stay in wet clothes ＿＿＿＿＿＿ of course you'll be ill.
4 It was ＿＿＿＿＿＿ a poor film ＿＿＿＿＿＿ I came out after half an hour.
5 ＿＿＿＿＿＿ Darren will finish his work today ＿＿＿＿＿＿ he will not play football.
6 The book was ＿＿＿＿＿＿ good ＿＿＿＿＿＿ I finished it before I went to sleep.

Spelling

Here is a list of twenty-five words of which *ten* are spelt incorrectly. Find them and write them out correctly.

deceive	definate	modern	foreign	beginning
saucer	memory	cinema	seperate	Wedensday
electricity	Febuary	anxious	creature	presant
sieze	language	eigth	nuisance	ordinary
interrupted	neccessary	skillful	beleive	wriggled

Singular

Rewrite these sentences in the **singular**.
1 The windows have been cleaned.
2 These boys wish to play chess.
3 We were hoping to finish the paintings last Monday.
4 The ladies checked their watches.
5 The policewomen arrested the thieves.
6 We don't think you can catch the mice.
7 Chimpanzees are intelligent animals.
8 Our cousins are coming on holiday with our family.

Completing sentences

Complete the following by adding interesting phrases which tell us **where** something took place.
1 We planted several trees _____ .
2 There was a raging fire _____ .
3 There were many fish _____ .
4 The exhausted climbers spent the night _____ .
5 The damaged aircraft was forced to land _____ .
6 A new bus shelter was built _____ .
7 The football international match took place _____ .
8 I saw a helicopter rescue the fishermen _____ .

Spelling

All these answers have **our** in them.

1 not sweet to taste __ o u r
2 tennis is played on a __ o u r __
3 a sheltered place where ships are safe __ __ __ __ o u r
4 someone who writes for newspapers or magazines
__ o u r __ __ __ __ __
5 to help someone to keep on trying __ __ __ o u r __ __ __
6 a person who lives near you __ __ __ __ __ __ o u r
7 going from one place to another __ o u r __ __ __
8 covering to protect the body from injury __ __ __ o u r

Joining phrases

Join the following pairs of phrases by choosing the most suitable word from those in the brackets.

1 She was very ill (but, and, so) we phoned for the doctor.
2 It is very late (so, but, and) we can still catch the last bus.
3 We must leave now (and, so, or) we shall miss the train.
4 She may be very poor (so, but, or) she is genuine.
5 I have my kagoul (so, but, because) it doesn't matter if it rains.
6 You make a model your way (although, and, so) I'll make one my way.
7 Sally is a fast runner (because, so, but) she didn't win the race.
8 Darren is very unhappy (but, because, although) he has lost his dog.
9 You don't need to come with us (so, unless, but) you wish to.
10 Heather toasted the bread (but, because, while) Edna boiled the eggs.

Incorrect sentences

Rewrite these sentences correctly.

1 She ran home as quick as she could.
2 My radio battery is wore out.
3 There is a cat and a dog on our front garden.
4 The steeplejack has broke his leg.
5 My fingers ache and I cannot write no more.
6 "Please pass me them books," said Graham.
7 "I seen the boy run over the field," said the caretaker.
8 The teacher thought Michael done it.
9 Wasn't they pleased when they knew we was coming.
10 Every one of us have an equal chance off reaching the final.

Rhyming words

Among these twenty words there are *five sets* of **rhyming words**—*four* words in each set. Write out the five sets.

made	home	become	cheer	played
toes	some	near	dome	froze
weighed	foam	crumb	grows	raid
smear	comb	glum	chose	sphere

Questions

Write *two sets* of questions—one **serious** and the other **humorous**—to which the following would be reasonable answers.

1 Three and a half kilometres.
2 Either a bull or a cow.
3 Maths, science and geography.
4 Follow the road to the traffic lights and turn right.
5 Black and white stripes.
6 At midnight.
7 As soon as I have eaten my breakfast.
8 Probably a hockey player or a golfer.
9 It landed in the main street.
10 Jamaica or New Zealand.

Homonyms

Complete the following by choosing the correct word from the brackets.

1 Cynthia has _____ her hair blonde.   (died, dyed)
2 Female sheep are _____ .   (ewes, yews)
3 Sam _____ us about his fishing holiday.   (told, tolled)
4 Brian was _____ for speeding on his motorbike.   (find, fined)
5 Dad has _____ many kinds of vegetable seeds this year. (sown, sewn)
6 The _____ is a part of your foot.   (heel, heal)
7 Our church bells were _____ for the harvest festival. (told, tolled)
8 Mum has _____ two badges on my anorak.   (sown, sewn)
9 We are going to football _____ tonight.   (practise, practice)
10 I must _____ shooting with my right foot.   (practise, practice)

Similes

Complete these **similes**—the answers are all *animals*.

1 as stubborn as _____
2 as playful as _____
3 as frisky as _____
4 as poor as _____
5 as strong as _____
6 as gentle as _____
7 as proud as _____
8 as blind as _____
9 as swift as _____
10 as wise as _____

Pronouns

Rewrite the following sentences by forming the correct words from those given in brackets.

 1 What have you done with (you) fishing rod?
 2 On (he) return home Peter could not open the door.
 3 Tom's bicycle is clean but (I) is very dirty.
 4 Our friends have a new car. Ours is smaller than (they).
 5 I have mislaid my dictionary. Will you lend me (you)?
 6 The bus was damaged but (it) passengers were unhurt.
 7 Alex and Graham left on their journey after saying goodbye to (they) friends.
 8 Jenny wanted to borrow (I) bicycle to go to the shops.
 9 Those aren't your football boots. They are (me).
10 (We) netball team won all (it) matches in the league.

your or you're

Complete these sentences by writing either **your** or **you're**.
 1 Please tell me when _____ ready to begin.
 2 You should help _____ mother more often.
 3 Do _____ feet ache when _____ running the cross country?
 4 If _____ coming, bring _____ bat and wickets.
 5 I think _____ improving but _____ still not ready to take _____ place in the team.

Vocabulary

Write out the word which is **out of place** in these groups of words.
 1 hamster rabbit cat rat squirrel
 2 regulate adjust modify vary replace
 3 conclude cease halt commence terminate
 4 brother nephew cousin son father
 5 speed rush hurry stroll hasten
 6 climb descend decline drop fall
 7 trip voyage hotel journey excursion
 8 daffodil rose crocus tulip snowdrop
 9 hail rain sleet snow heat
10 pine cedar holly ash yew

Verbs

A Make a list of **verbs** in these sentences.

1 She offered to lend me her tennis racket.
2 Andrew ran well and finished second.
3 Annette called at her aunty's before she went to school.
4 My dog comes to me when I whistle.
5 "Run away and play in the park," suggested Dad.
6 In the morning Derek ate his breakfast, then dug the garden, cut the grass and trimmed the hedge.
7 "Come and read to me," said the teacher.
8 The trawler was tossed about in the storm and struck the rocks and sank.
9 Fiona rode her bicycle to school but she fell off and cut her arm.
10 The tall striker swerved past the centre half and scored a brilliant goal.

B Write the **verbs** which match the following meanings. The first letter of each verb is given.

1 to cry   w_____
2 to make better again   c_____
3 to go on foot   w_____
4 to feel   t_____
5 to go up in the air   r_____
6 to make a noise like a duck
   q_____
7 to hit with the foot   k_____
8 to walk through water
   w_____
9 to turn round and round
   t_____
10 to hear carefully   l_____

11 to turn like a wheel   r_____
12 to do as you are told   o_____
13 to repair   m_____
14 to hold tightly   g_____
15 to end; to complete   f_____
16 to spread or open out
   u_____
17 to take away   s_____
18 to buy   p_____
19 to eat in small bites   n_____
20 to give up   s_____

Adjectives

A Write out the **adjectives** in these sentences.

1 The downcast team walked off the muddy field after losing their first match.
2 The two considerate children helped the elderly lady across the busy street.
3 Continuous rain made the holiday beach a dismal sight.
4 The four experienced climbers succeeded in climbing the sheer, slippery rock-face.
5 An impressive welcome awaited the three triumphant American balloonists after their successful crossing of the vast Atlantic.
6 Heavy grey clouds darkened the sky and torrential rain followed quickly to ruin the exciting game of cricket.

B Write down the strongest **adjective** in each group.

1 sore, uncomfortable, tender, agonizing, painful
2 disobedient, naughty, wicked, mischievous, incorrect
3 fine, good, great, incomparable, fair, valuable
4 sizeable, big, large, great, giant, colossal
5 interesting, gorgeous, pretty, handsome, charming

C Make the meanings of the following nouns more interesting by adding **two adjectives** to each.

e.g. dog ⟶ a black, shaggy dog

1 holiday	6 street	11 room
2 tree	7 smell	12 fire
3 mountain	8 film	13 wind
4 dream	9 cat	14 neighbour
5 friend	10 hobby	15 sunset

Spelling

Here is a list of twenty-five words. *Twelve* are spelt incorrectly. Find them
and write them spelt correctly.

library	secondry	generous	leisure	minature
excitement	parallel	calender	marvelous	disagree
dissappear	exaggerate	temprature	interfere	parliment
poisonous	adress	detatch	cautious	courageous
choclate	breakable	terrific	cuboard	miscellanous

Comparing adjectives

e.g. big, bigger, biggest   beautiful, more beautiful, most beautiful.
Complete the table.

positive	comparative	superlative
1 tall		
2 safe		
3 heavy		
4 noisy		
5 honest		
6 intelligent		
7 good		
8 old		
9 bad		
10 thoughtful		

Vocabulary

A Write *one word only* for each of the following.

1 go into _____
2 go up _____
3 go back _____
4 go down _____
5 go on hands and knees _____
6 go forward _____
7 go away _____
8 go after _____

B Complete the following to make interesting sentences.

1 Arriving at the airport, we _____ .
2 Browsing round the market, the old lady _____ .
3 Looking through the door, Roger saw _____ .
4 Seizing him by the trousers, _____ .
5 Running down the street, Sonia _____ .

Comprehension

David's feet were no longer part of him. When he himself cared no more, his feet followed their own path independently, stealing along noiselessly, confidently, guiding his body so that he kept to the shadows and avoided obstacles, stopping him in time, or urging him on whenever he felt he would rather lie down and wait till he was caught. And his feet had carried him over the bridge.

He clenched his teeth. "Salonica!" he whispered and went on repeating the word over and over again to himself until it seemed to fill his brain. "Go south till you reach Salonica. Think of nothing else!"

At that moment the sound of a car pulling up caused him to stiffen. Was he far enough from the road? Then he heard voices. He was so terrified he nearly jumped out of his skin. He was quite unused to the sound of voices by this time; the last he had heard were the guard's and the man's.

But these were different, and they were coming nearer. David relaxed completely so that he would make as little noise as possible, and as he did so he thought that in a moment all would be over—everything.

The men sat down a little way off and lit cigarettes, and it gradually dawned upon David that they were not looking for him at all. He began to listen to what they were saying. He found it difficult to follow them since their speech differed from the man's, but after a while David was able to distinguish words that were familiar to him. They drove a delivery van, like the men who brought supplies to the camp. They were arguing now, but with no great heat: one of them wanted to drive on, and the other wanted to visit someone first in the town David had seen nearby. In the end he got his way; the first man said he would go with him, but only for half an hour as it was a long way home.

Like an echo of his own thoughts, David caught the word 'Salonica'!

From *I am David* by Anne Holm
Reprinted by permission of Methuen Children's Books Ltd

1a What place was David trying to reach?
  b In which direction did this place lie?
2 Would you say David had been travelling for a long time or not? Give a
  reason for your answer.
3 David appears to be an escaped prisoner. Find two facts from the
  passage which suggest this.
4 Why was David terrified when he heard voices?
5 What made him realise that the men weren't looking for him?
6 Why did David find it difficult to understand what the men were saying?
7 Where did David think he had seen the van before?
8 What sound caused David to 'stiffen'?
9 Quote three phrases from the passage which suggest that David's feet
  were moving of their own accord.
10 When and where do you think David's adventure took place?
11 Give a title to this extract.
12 In your own words explain the following phrases.
  stealing along
  it gradually dawned upon David
  with no great heat
  like an echo of his own thoughts
13 Write sentences to show that you know the meaning of these words.
  avoid   relax   distinguish
  clench   differ
14 Pick out the following from the passage.
  a three adverbs   **d** three pronouns
  b three prepositions   **e** three verbs
  c three common nouns **f** three adjectives

Verbs

Complete each sentence by choosing the most suitable **verb**. Do not use said.

1 "Simon Aitken is the winner of the cross country cup," _____ the principal.
2 "Don't make a sound or they'll find us," _____ Ruth.
3 "Stop! The bridge has collapsed," _____ the policeman.
4 "I'll win all the races, you'll see," _____ the boy.
5 "It would be much safer if you followed the path," _____ the farmer.
6 "Yes, it was me. I broke the window," _____ Tim.
7 "This class is too noisy. Also you are lazy," _____ the teacher.
8 "I shall have to think carefully about that," _____ Fiona.

Rhyming words

In each of these lines of words pick out the word that **does not** rhyme with the word in bold type.

1 **weight**	hate	wait	height	freight	fête
2 **drain**	main	feign	mane	same	lane
3 **dough**	sew	doe	bough	flow	so
4 **steak**	stake	ache	flake	streak	snake
5 **pair**	pier	pear	tare	fair	snare
6 **berth**	earth	worth	birth	dearth	hearth
7 **rein**	sane	rain	reign	pain	maim
8 **stone**	known	frown	sewn	loan	phone

Homonyms

For each of the following words write another word which **sounds exactly the same** but is spelt differently.

1 steel _____   5 boy _____   9 tale _____
2 meet _____   6 waste _____   10 missed _____
3 right _____   7 bear _____   11 foul _____
4 hose _____   8 reed _____   12 guilt _____

Use each of the words you have found in a sentence to show that you understand what each one means.

Prepositions

Write out the **prepositions** in these sentences.

1 The farmer was angry with the boys who had damaged his fence.
2 Christine was asked to write about her favourite sport.
3 The frightened horse jumped over the five-barred gate.
4 The driver stood beside his damaged car.
5 I thanked my aunty for her present.
6 The sweets were shared among the whole class.
7 Jane ran past the finishing line in second place.
8 Clive's golf clubs are different from Paul's.
9 I sat between Gareth and Malcolm.
10 The policeman chased the thief through the narrow streets.

Joining sentences

Join the following pairs of sentences by choosing from

but	or	so
which		while

1 We stayed at the hotel. It overlooks the bay.
2 A man fell in the river. We were swimming.
3 Will you have lemonade? Do you prefer shandy?
4 This story is very strange. It really happened.
5 The wind and rain stopped the cricket match. We decided to go home.

# of or off

Choose **of** or **off** to complete these sentences.

1 I saw the old man fall _____ the bus.
2 One _____ my friends caught a large pike.
3 As soon as the plane took _____ several _____ us felt ill.
4 Two _____ Mr. Aitken's cows ran _____ down the road.
5 _____ course you will be goalkeeper unless the game is _____ .

Synonyms

Write down words which are **similar** in meaning to these.

1 rough _____
2 conceal _____
3 correct _____
4 prohibit _____
5 imitate _____
6 bravery _____
7 empty _____
8 circular _____
9 start _____
10 feeble _____
11 guard _____
12 aid _____

Prepositions

The **prepositions** in bold type in these sentences are not the correct ones.
Rewrite the sentences using the correct prepositions.

1 The reward was shared equally **between** Paul, Simon and Andrew.
2 Sally was eating her lunch all **to** herself.
3 The watchman came **of** duty at 7.00 am.
4 Eight comes **before** seven and nine.
5 Terry ran **beyond** the winning post in record time.
6 Do you live **at** a town or village?
7 A rabbit is different in several ways **than** a hare.
8 Heather rested her elbows **onto** the desk.
9 The food was shared equally **among** the two dogs.
10 Patrick may not be **to** school this afternoon.
11 Pour the water **in** the bowl.
12 Mary hasn't received any letters **off** her friends.

Analogies

Complete these analogies which all deal with **gender**.

1 Masculine is to _____ as male is to female.
2 Prince is to princess as _____ is to queen.
3 Father is to _____ as mother is to daughter.
4 _____ is to Mrs. as he is to she.
5 Boy is to girl as man is to _____ .
6 Uncle is to aunt as nephew is to _____ .
7 Author is to authoress as _____ is to waitress.
8 She is to he as her is to _____ .
9 Duke is to _____ as lord is to lady.
10 Brother is to sister as bridegroom is to _____ .
11 Sir is to madam as _____ is to witch.
12 Widow is to _____ as heroine is to hero.

there or their

Complete these sentences by writing **there** or **their**.

1 The two boys cleaned ＿＿＿＿ bicycles.
2 ＿＿＿＿ were crowds of people watching the carnival.
3 Gareth and Alison were ＿＿＿＿ with ＿＿＿＿ two friends.
4 The motorists were annoyed because ＿＿＿＿ cars had been damaged in the car park.
5 ＿＿＿＿ are too many children who have forgotten ＿＿＿＿ homework.
6 Do you think ＿＿＿＿ is any chance of Tracy and Deborah going on the coach trip with ＿＿＿＿ friends?

Adverbs from nouns

Complete the following sentences by using an **adverb** formed from the **noun** in the brackets.

1 Pat played the piano (skill).
2 The climbers proceeded (caution) across the glacier.
3 The doctor cared (devotion) for his patients.
4 Stephanie answered the questions (sense).
5 Our school (generosity) supported the earthquake disaster appeal.

Completing sentences

Complete these sentences by choosing the correct word from the brackets.

1 Each of the boys did (their, his) best to complete the climb.
2 Every one of those houses (has, have) something wrong with (it, them).
3 Each of the hotel bedrooms (has, have) (its, their) own balcony.
4 Every one of the yachts had capsized before (it, they) finished the course.
5 Each of the labradors (has, have) been chosen to train as a guide dog.

Opposites

Write down the **opposite** of these words.

1 late ＿＿＿＿
2 up ＿＿＿＿
3 different ＿＿＿＿
4 entrance ＿＿＿＿
5 friend ＿＿＿＿
6 always ＿＿＿＿
7 from ＿＿＿＿
8 success ＿＿＿＿
9 out ＿＿＿＿
10 under ＿＿＿＿
11 short ＿＿＿＿
12 deep ＿＿＿＿

Direct speech

Write out these sentences, using **inverted commas** where required.

1 Help! she screamed. The boat is sinking.
2 Please open the window, Mr. Allinson said. I find it stuffy.
3 If you call me mean once more, warned Malcolm, I'll hit you.
4 Excuse me, Mrs. Thomas, said Peter, but I think you have left your umbrella.
5 In a quiet voice Lucy asked, May I have my ball back?
6 Stay where you are! the farmer shouted to us.
7 I am very grateful for the invitation, said Michael, but I am afraid I shan't be able to accept.
8 His mother told him, You must be back by nine o'clock.
9 Have you seen my dog? the old man inquired. It ran off early this morning.
10 Yes, I did eat all the cake, admitted Andrew, but I was very hungry.

Spelling

All these words are spelt incorrectly. Write them spelt correctly.

1 peice
2 allso
3 recieve
4 quantaty
5 invisable
6 goverment
7 excitment
8 visiter
9 libary
10 alltogether
11 differant
12 developement

Opposites—prefixes

Write the **opposites** of these words by adding a **prefix**.

1 sincere
2 perfect
3 lawful
4 sense
5 possible
6 order
7 truthful
8 allow
9 welcome
10 honour
11 responsible
12 complete

Use each of the opposites you have formed in a sentence to show that you understand what each one means.

Sayings

In each of these sentences rewrite the **everyday saying** in bold type to show that you understand its meaning.

1 The boy **showed a clean pair of heels** when the watchman spotted him.
2 Are you ever **at a loose end** during the holidays?
3 If Jimmy doesn't alter he'll become **a good for nothing**.
4 It was an excellent game; the only **fly in the ointment** was that our team lost.
5 My Aunty Ellen visits us only **once in a blue moon**.
6 I think it's about time those two **buried the hatchet**.
7 **My heart was in my mouth** as I watched the trapeze artists at the circus.
8 Barry decided to **make a clean breast of it** to his teacher.
9 I hope Dad doesn't **throw cold water** on our party plans.
10 I'm very pleased to know that Jenny is now **up to the mark**.

Completing sentences

Complete the following by adding interesting phrases which tell **why** something happened.

1 The helicopter could not land on the rig _____ .
2 Douglas was unable to fasten his suitcase _____ .
3 The Jumbo jet failed to take off _____ .
4 Sarah didn't return the book to the library _____ .
5 None of us saw the bridge collapse _____ .
6 Oliver was very upset _____ .
7 There weren't any fish in the lake _____ .
8 The postman couldn't get an answer _____ .
9 The climbers failed to reach the summit _____ .
10 Our caretaker was very annoyed _____ .

Spelling

These words end in either **ible** or **able**.

1 that which can be seen
2 showing good sense
3 to be trusted or relied upon
4 awful: frightful
5 easy to carry

Picture vocabulary

Give the names of these items worn on the feet. Who would wear them? Write an interesting sentence about each.

Noun groups

In the following list of nouns there are five names of **parts of the body**, five **animals** and five **buildings**. There are also five words that do not belong to any of the three groups.

Make a list of the nouns *in the correct groups*.

bank	rounders	badger	skull	net
school	skill	ankle	bat	wrist
factory	hotel	arm	bark	falcon
tower	wasp	scoop	neck	snail

Sayings

Explain what is meant by these **sayings**.

1 sink or swim
2 walls have ears
3 dead beat
4 out of his depth
5 sit on the fence
6 take the rough with the smooth
7 let bygones be bygones
8 a feather in your cap
9 blow your own trumpet
10 let sleeping dogs lie

Punctuation

Write out these sentences using **inverted commas** and other **necessary punctuation**.

1 heres philip lets ask him to come with us said bruce
2 does mr rigby still mend clocks inquired elaine
3 youre not always right you know said adrian
4 denise shouted to her mother will you answer the telephone
5 robert looked at the muddy field and said ill be surprised if we start the match
6 keep on practising marilyn urged her piano teacher you will master this difficult piece
7 where does britain obtain most of its rubber asked fred
8 is the soviet union one country asked hilary or is it a number of countries together
9 the pacific said mr brady is the largest of the worlds oceans
10 stop shouted the policeman you cant go down market street because theres a burst water main

Homonyms

A Write a word which is spelt differently but **sounds the same** as the following.

1 bridal _____	6 seen _____	11 draft _____
2 birth _____	7 mussel _____	12 vain _____
3 cereal _____	8 kernel _____	13 sword _____
4 prophet _____	9 paws _____	14 principle _____
5 waist _____	10 would _____	15 cheque _____

B Choose any *five* of your word pairs and write sentences to show that you understand their meanings.

whose or who's

Complete these sentences by writing either **whose** or **who's**.

1 Will you tell me _____ borrowed my pen?
2 _____ coming for a game of football?
3 Will you find out _____ book this is?
4 We met Kenny _____ sister swims for Scotland.
5 Do you know _____ coming on holiday with us?
6 _____ dog is that running across the road?
7 We saw an actor _____ often in programmes on television.
8 I saw Mr. Park, _____ house was damaged in a storm.

Prepositions

Complete these sentences with suitable **prepositions**.

1 My sister is very good _____ embroidery.
2 Are you pleased _____ your new car?
3 I know I can rely _____ you to help.
4 I am tired _____ playing chess every night.
5 A letter arrived _____ my friend in Canada yesterday.
6 Bernard apologised _____ the teacher for being late.
7 The cyclist was involved _____ an accident outside school.
8 The thirsty dog longed _____ a drink of water.

Vocabulary

Rewrite these sentences using a **better word** than got.

1 The fireman **got** on the roof to rescue the kitten.
2 When we finally **got to** the station the train had gone.
3 Julie soon **got better** from her illness.
4 We **got back** from the cinema at ten o'clock.
5 The passengers **got on** the aeroplane one hour late.
6 The cook **got ready** an appetising meal.

Collective nouns

Complete the following by choosing a suitable **collective noun**.

1 a _____ of bees
2 a squadron of _____
3 a _____ of books
4 a host of _____
5 a bench of _____

6 an _____ of soldiers
7 a _____ of rabbits
8 a brood of _____
9 an _____ of poems

Write the **initial letters** of the words you have used. They should spell a Spanish city.

Proverbs

Complete these **proverbs**.

One _____ doesn't make a summer.
Don't put all your _____ in one basket.
A _____ is as good as a mile.
_____ makes the heart grow fonder.
_____ is the best policy.
One good _____ deserves another.

Write the **initial letters** of the words you have used. Reverse their order and you should have the name of an English river.

Opposites

Write the **opposites** of the following words. The last letters of the words you need are given.

1 minimum   _____m
2 straight   _____t
3 permanent   _____y
4 pretty   _____y
5 true   _____e
6 no   _____s

7 wise   _____h
8 hollow   _____d
9 victory   _____t
10 senior   _____r
11 opaque   _____t
12 barren   _____e

Take the letter of the alphabet which comes immediately before each initial letter of the words you have made. What is the message this gives?

Comprehension

On the verge of a wood within a mile of the town of Ashby was an extensive meadow. The ground sloped gradually down on all sides to a level bottom, and was enclosed for the lists with strong palisades, forming an oblong space a quarter of a mile in length and about half as broad. Strong wooden gates, each wide enough to admit two horsemen riding abreast, afforded entry for the combatants at the northern and southern ends of the lists. At each of these two heralds were stationed and a strong body of men-at-arms for maintaining order.

On a platform beyond the southern entrance were pitched five magnificent pavilions, adorned with pennons of russet and black, the chosen colours of the five knights' challengers. The northern access to the lists terminated in a similar entrance of thirty feet in breadth, outside which was a large enclosed space for such knights as intended to enter the lists with the challengers. Behind were placed tents for armourers, farriers, and other attendants ready to give their services wherever they might be necessary.

The exterior of the lists was occupied by temporary galleries for those lords and ladies who were expected to attend the tournament. A narrow space between these galleries and the lists gave accommodation for spectators of a better degree than the mere vulgar. The latter arranged themselves upon banks of turf prepared for the purpose, while many hundreds had perched themselves on the branches of trees around the meadow; even the steeple of a church at some distance was crowded with spectators.

One gallery in the very centre of the eastern side of the lists, exactly opposite to the spot where the shock of the combat was to take place, was raised higher than the others, more richly decorated, and graced by a sort of throne and canopy, on which the royal arms were emblazoned.

From *Ivanhoe* by Sir Walter Scott

1 What were the colours of the challengers?
2 Name all the viewing points for the spectators.
3 Who would keep order?
4 What are farriers?
5 What work would be done by an armourer?
6 What were the duties of the heralds?
7 Why was the royal gallery situated in that particular place?
8 What is the 'shock of the combat'?
9 Which spectators watched from the banks of turf?
10 How do you know that this event was very well attended?
11 Find the meanings of these words.
   palisades   pennons   gallery   canopy
12 Find words in the passage which mean the same as the following.
   a allowed   **d** not permanent
   b outside   **e** ended
   c decorated   **f** edge
13 In what century do you think the tournament could have taken place?
14 Draw a plan of the tournament field and mark all the important details.
15 Give a title to this extract.

Verbs

Use each of these **verbs** in sentences of your own.

1 limped	5 descended	9 complained
2 unfolded	6 demolished	10 believed
3 attracted	7 beckoned	11 scrambled
4 encouraged	8 challenged	12 struggled

Possession

Use the apostrophe (') to show ownership.

1 a hairdresser for men
2 the paints of the artist
3 a library for children
4 the toys of the babies
5 a concert for pensioners

6 a corner for pets
7 the voice of the singer
8 the tennis rackets of the girls
9 the cricket bat owned by James
10 the feathers of the geese

Silent letters

The answers to these clues all contain a **silent letter**. Underline the silent letter in each word.

1 unable to speak   d _ _ _
2 Malta is an   i _ _ _ _ _
3 a fish with pink flesh   s _ _ _ _ _
4 to hear carefully   l _ _ _ _ _
5 a dwarf or a goblin   g _ _ _ _
6 not right   w _ _ _ _

7 a war plane   b _ _ _ _ _
8 a joint in the fingers   k _ _ _ _ _ _
9 a tree growing in hot countries   p _ _ _
10 a large cat with spots   l _ _ _ _ _ _
11 where things are stored   d _ _ _ _ _
12 serious; sincere   s _ _ _ _ _

Nouns from verbs

Form **nouns** from these verbs.

1 arrive	6 donate	11 capture
2 punish	7 memorise	12 applaud
3 move	8 destroy	13 believe
4 complain	9 imagine	14 alter
5 depart	10 enlarge	15 conclude

Answers

Page 2 Picture vocabulary
1 kangaroo **2** walrus **3** bat **4** beaver
5 whale **6** tiger **7** platypus **8** skunk
9 elephant **10** rhino **11** giraffe **12** polar
bear **13** gorilla **14** koala **15** zebra
16 squirrel **17** camel **18** mouse **19** hippo
20 porcupine

Page 3 Pronouns
A 1 he **2** We, they **3** He, me, he **4** I, her,
she, me **5** them, me **6** She, they, her
7 you, him **8** They, him, they, us **9** She, it,
me, her **10** He, he, it
B 1 hers **2** mine **3** ours **4** his **5** theirs
6 yours
C 1 they **2** him **3** it **4** us **5** you, her

Page 4 Alphabetical order
A 1 tank, tent, thermometer, tiger, tractor
2 pan, pity, plum, polish, pull, pygmy
3 hawk, help, high, hobby, huge, hymn
4 fair, fear, field, flat, foot, funny
5 wash, week, whirl, witch, worm, wrote
B 1 cage, calendar, camel, castle, caterpillar
2 baboon, banana, barley, basket, bath, bay
3 factory, fail, fall, family, fan, fast
4 habit, hair, ham, harp, hatch, hawk
5 meat, meet, mellow, mend, merge,
message
C 1 forbid, forfeit, forget, fork, form, forward
2 patch, paternal, path, patience, patrol,
patter
3 cancel, candid, cane, canoe, canvas,
canyon
4 manager, mane, mankind, manly, manor,
mansion

Page 5 Picture vocabulary
1 bicycle **2** hot air balloon **3** van **4** sledge
5 hovercraft **6** plane **7** car **8** boat **9** bus
10 helicopter **11** canoe **12** train **13** tanker
14 shuttle **15** motorbike
Check your child's five descriptions.

Page 6 Vocabulary – associations
A 1 fish **2** army **3** history **4** storage
5 aircraft **6** birds **7** fruit **8** artist **9** water
10 oil **11** ship **12** grapes
B 1 headteacher **2** sister **3** captain
4 principal **5** keeper **6** director **7** governor
8 president **9** editor **10** matron **11** judge
12 conductor
C 1 dictionary **2** autobiography **3** atlas

4 diary **5** anthology **6** log book **7** scrap
book **8** encyclopaedia **9** telephone
directory **10** album

Page 7 Verbs – sounds
A 1 – 6 Check that your child has chosen an
appropriate verb for each sentence.
B 1 – 8 Check that your child's sound words
are suitable.
C 1 – 8 Check that your child's words are
suitable.
D 1 – 4 Check your child's sentences.

Page 8 Spelling
1 weight **2** niece **3** neighbour **4** shriek
5 mischief **6** deceive **7** retrieve **8** ceiling
9 foreign **10** reindeer **11** ancient **12** receipt
13 seize **14** cashier **15** conceit
16 chief

Vocabulary
1 – 6 Check that your child's words are
suitable for their sentence.

Punctuation
1 Clive, Paul and Craig play golf every
Saturday and Sunday.
2 Mrs Marsden told Janet to take the cakes
to Aunty Margaret.
3 In our Easter holidays we went to London
and saw Buckingham Palace and the Bank
of England.
4 His friends, who were becoming anxious,
telephoned Leeds police station.
A policeman soon arrived.
5 Trevor Francis became the first one million
pound footballer when he was transferred
from Birmingham City to Nottingham
Forest.
6 For Sunday lunch Bob and Roger had
pork chops, cabbage, carrots and roast
potatoes.

Page 9 Abbreviations
1 The National Society for the Prevention of
Cruelty to Children
2 Royal Automobile Club
3 United States of America
4 Royal National Lifeboat Institute
5 Company
6 British Rail
7 Master of Ceremonies
8 Youth Opportunity Centre
9 Royal National Institute for the Blind
10 World Wildlife Fund
11 International Monetary Fund

12 North Atlantic Treaty Organisation
13 British Summer Time
14 United Kingdom
15 Air Force Cross
16 Genetically Modified

Opposites

1 arrive
2 often
3 poverty
4 innocent
5 gradual
6 maximum
7 fertile
8 advance
9 minority
10 still
11 illegal
12 external

Synonyms

1 begin/start 2 dear 3 outside 4 cure
5 huge 6 level 7 savage/cruel
8 cheeky 9 allow 10 forsake 11 copy
12 clear/translucent

Homonyms

1 saw or soar 2 meddle 3 quay 4 wrap
5 route 6 weight 7 bridal 8 peddle 9 aisle
10 principal 11 dough 12 sealing

Page 10 Adjectives

A 1 – 10 Check that your child's adjectives
are suitable to complete the sentence.
B 1 gigantic 2 brilliant 3 beautiful
4 miserable 5 icy 6 towering
C 1 – 10 Check your child's adjectives are
opposite in meaning to those given.

Page 11 Spelling and vocabulary

A 1 seaweed 2 shoal 3 submarine 4 shark
5 scuba diver
B 1 exercise 2 explored 3 extended
4 extracted 5 expensive
C 1 fruit 2 vegetable 3 shape 4 metal
5 ocean
D 1 – 5 Check that your child's words are
suitable.

Page 12 Vocabulary

A 1 stetson – a cowboy 2 mitre – a bishop
3 hard hat – miner 4 wig - judge 5 fire
helmet - fireman 6 space helmet -
astronaut 7 nurse's hat - nurse
B 1 grains 2 abbreviations 3 freshwater
fish 4 surnames 5 rodents 6 insects
7 herbs 8 woods
C 1 office 2 galley 3 darkroom
4 safe or vault 5 cabin 6 cell

Page 13 Indirect speech

1 Danny said that his football boots needed
new laces.
2 The policeman said to my dad that he
wasn't allowed to park his car in this street.
3 Heather asked if the train to Walsall had
gone.
4 Aunty Shirley said to me that she hoped I
liked my birthday present.
5 I asked the librarian if she had a copy of
Oliver Twist.
6 Marian said that she goes swimming
twice a week.
7 Mr. Rigby snapped at Brian that he was
afraid he wasn't working hard enough to
pass the exam.
8 The teacher asked Norma if she would
please bring the tape recorder.
9 George said that I was a slow coach and
we would miss the bus if we didn't hurry.
10 Mildred said to George that she was
sorry but she was running as fast as she
could.

Present and past tense

1 gave 2 knew 3 caught 4 felt 5 left
6 swam 7 struck 8 laid 9 began 10 drank
11 throw 12 forget 13 build 14 ring
15 steal 16 bring 17 hold 18 shake
19 drive 20 fly

Page 14 Direct speech

1 Simon asked, "How tall are you?"
2 My mother asked, "Are you ready for
tea?"
3 Elizabeth shouted to Susan, "Be quick!"
4 The mechanic told Mr. Barnes, "Your car
will be ready on Tuesday."
5 Pat's mother asked her, "Have you
finished your homework?"
6 Paul told his dad, "I've been chosen to
play for the school cricket team."
7 Derek asked Mark, "Do you want to go
fishing?"
8 Mrs. Bladen told her son, Andrew, "You
must not miss the last bus home."
9 Harry Cox shouted, "I'm trapped on my
roof!"
10 Mr. Green asked David, "Clean the
windows and brush the floor."

Incorrect sentences

1 The dog and the cat **were** lying on the carpet.
2 Malcolm **taught** me to play badminton.
3 Was it her or him **who** spoke to you?
4 Dawn could not see her dog **anywhere**.
5 You can **borrow** my bicycle if you're careful.
6 Patrick **caught two** perch in the canal.
7 The reward was **shared** among the three boys.
8 Have you **spoken** to your father?
9 My brother is taller than **I**.
10 Neither the boys nor the girls **have** finished **their** work.

Page 15 Picture story

Check that your child's story explains what is happening in the pictures.

Page 16 Contractions

1 must not 2 that is 3 I will 4 we have
5 you are 6 who would 7 where is
8 would not 9 she will 10 they have
11 will not 12 they will 13 there would
14 it is 15 we will

Vocabulary

1 did 2 saw 3 who 4 I 5 those 6 teach
7 where, were 8 seen, saw 9 me
10 too, to, two

Adjectives

1 warmer 2 less 3 most, honest
4 cleverer 5 cosiest 6 more generous

Page 17 Plurals

1 Yesterday the workmen repaired the roofs.
2 I saw calves, horses, geese, and donkeys on the farm.
3 The policewomen caught the thieves in the act.
4 The old ladies twisted their ankles on the stony beaches.
5 The boys fell off the rocks and hurt themselves.
6 My cousins came to see us last weekend.
7 The girls' pencils were in the boxes.
8 The school plays weren't very well acted.
9 The postmen delivered letters and parcels to houses in the valleys.
10 We do not think you understand the problems.

Spelling

1 We all laughed at the puppy's **behaviour**.

2 Janet was very **tearful** when she fell off her bicycle.
3 I saw the rabbit **disappear** down that hole.
4 Neither John nor Betty has **completed** the work.
5 The policeman **seized** the frightened dog.
6 **Although** he was near exhaustion, Bill finished the race.
7 Heather replied **sensibly** to the teacher's questions.
8 There was a **beautiful** display of roses in the entrance hall.
9 In warm weather Gaynor **always** wears sandals.
10 Mum knitted a **woollen** jersey.

Page 18 Vocabulary – verb association

A 1 to conceal – hide 2 to demolish – pull or tear down; destroy 3 to substitute – replace one thing or person with another 4 to suppress – put an end to; stop by force 5 to excavate – scoop out; uncover by digging 6 to investigate – search into; examine closely 7 to erupt – burst forth 8 to refine – make pure
B 1 suppressed 2 erupted 3 excavated 4 refined 5 substituted
C 1 – 5 Check your child's answers.

Page 19 Spelling and vocabulary

A 1 pianist 2 typist 3 scientist 4 novelist 5 parachutist 6 ventriloquist 7 soloist 8 optimist
B 1 attic 2 attempt 3 attack 4 attractive 5 attach
C 1 puncture 2 temperature 3 capture 4 furniture 5 torture
D 1 quarrel 2 mirror 3 surrender 4 terrier 5 quarry

Page 20 Analogies

1 stable 2 fur 3 trumpet 4 ewe 5 hare 6 sett 7 hiss 8 fish

Verbs

1 attack 2 suffering 3 enters 4 chase 5 persevere 6 fall

Vocabulary

1 applause 2 summit 3 spectator 4 famine 5 glacier 6 miser

Page 21 Pronouns

A 1 yourself 2 myself 3 yourselves 4 herself 5 himself
B 1 You – Steven 2 it – hurricane 3 they –

Paul and Sally **4** her – Jacqueline **5** me –
Mr. Morris
C 1 we **2** ourselves **3** they **4** theirs **5** us
6 mine **7** me **8** her/his **9** yourself **10** itself

Page 22 Contractions
1 Where've **2** doesn't **3** You'd **4** won't
5 can't **6** don't **7** I'd, you'd **8** shan't **9** I'll,
they're **10** They've, it's

Incorrect sentences
1 My brother **taught** me how to ride a bike.
2 Joan acted **well** in the play.
3 Seamus wouldn't give me **any** of his
toffees.
4 There **are** a lot of mountains in Austria.
5 Terry ran home as **quickly** as he could.
6 A man and his dog **were** waiting outside
the shop.
7 Beryl could not come **any** quicker.
8 Your fishing rod is different **from** mine.
9 The **better** team won the game.
10 The group **sang** the same song twice.
11 Poor Lesley couldn't remember **anything**.
12 Between you and **me**, I don't think he is
the right choice for captain.

Page 23 Vocabulary
1 feeling **2** exercising **3** gem **4** dwelling
5 time

Jumbled letters
1 owl **2** heron **3** kiwi **4** parrot **5** thrush
6 eagle

Associations
set A 1 photographer – camera **2** jockey –
saddle **3** referee – whistle **4** doctor –
stethoscope **5** conductor – baton
6 mechanic – spanner **7** decorator – brush
set B 1 actress – theatre **2** keeper –
lighthouse **3** chemist – laboratory
4 astronomer – observatory **5** typist – office
6 chef – kitchen **7** artist – studio

Page 24 Adverbs
A 1 regularly **2** dejectedly, loudly
3 now, soon **4** excitedly **5** angrily
6 everywhere, sadly **7** anywhere, sadly
8 always, well **9** away, loudly
10 once, frantically **11** never **12** twice
B These answers are just a guide. Check
that your child has used a suitable adverb in
each sentence.
1 thoroughly **2** badly **3** immediately
4 vividly **5** regularly **6** around **7** excitedly
8 softly **9** nastily **10** badly **11** attentively
12 suddenly **13** easily **14** around
15 greedily **16** patiently

Page 25 Opposites
1 Alan's invention was a **success**.
2 The yacht sailed through the **calm** seas.
3 Sarah checked the time as she **entered** the
office.
4 It was **impossible** for the mountain to be
climbed.
5 Bobby **denied** that he had left the tap
running.
6 The passengers were very **annoyed** when
the plane was delayed.
7 Our teacher was **encouraged** by our exam
results.
8 About one third of Jayne's answers were
incorrect.
9 The **minority** of our class come to school
by bus.
10 Tom helped his Dad to push the car
backwards.

Vocabulary
1 We managed to **extinguish** the fire.
2 Workmen have **erected** a bus shelter in
our street.
3 You can do it! Don't be **discouraged** by
their failure.
4 You will have to **save** some money for
your holidays.
5 The old lady couldn't **tolerate** the loud
noise of the machines any longer.
6 After losing a sail in a violent storm, the
yacht **entered** port for repairs.
7 Sally was **annoyed** by the way her friends
behaved towards her.
8 The football match was **postponed**
because of the frozen ground.

Page 26 Verbs
1 lubricate **2** narrate **3** meditate **4** cultivate
5 dilate **6** imitate **7** rotate **8** educate
9 relate **10** emigrate

Completing sentences
1 neither, nor **2** whether, or **3** If, then
4 such, that **5** Either, or **6** so, that

Spelling
definite, February, necessary, separate,
believe, Wednesday, present, seize, skilful,
eight

Page 27 Singular

1 The window has been cleaned.
2 This boy wishes to play chess.
3 I was hoping to finish the painting last Monday.
4 The lady checked her watch.
5 The policewoman arrested the thief.
6 I don't think you can catch the mouse.
7 The chimpanzee is an intelligent animal.
8 My cousin is coming on holiday with my family.

Completing sentences

1 – 8 Check that your child's answers explain where the action is taking place.

Spelling

1 sour 2 court 3 harbour 4 journalist 5 encourage 6 neighbour 7 journey 8 armour

Page 28 Joining phrases

1 so 2 but 3 or 4 but 5 so 6 and 7 but 8 because 9 unless 10 while

Incorrect sentences

1 She ran home as **quickly** as she could.
2 My radio battery is **worn** out.
3 There is a cat and a dog **in** our front garden.
4 The steeplejack has **broken** his leg.
5 My fingers ache and I cannot write **any** more.
6 "Please pass me **those** books," said Graham.
7 "I **saw** the boy run over the field," said the caretaker.
8 The teacher thought Michael **did** it.
9 **Weren't** they pleased when they knew we **were** coming?
10 Every one of us **has** an equal chance **of** reaching the final.

Rhyming words

made, weighed, played, raid; toes, grows, chose, froze; some, become, crumb, glum; smear, near, cheer, sphere; home, foam, comb, dome

Page 29 Questions

1 – 10 Check your child's answers.

Homonyms

1 dyed 2 ewes 3 told 4 fined 5 sown 6 heal 7 tolled 8 sewn 9 practice 10 practise

Similes

1 a mule 2 a kitten 3 a lamb 4 a church mouse 5 an ox 6 a dove 7 a peacock 8 a bat 9 a deer 10 an owl

Page 30 Pronouns

1 your 2 his 3 mine 4 theirs 5 yours 6 its 7 their 8 my 9 mine 10 our, its

your or you're

1 you're 2 your 3 your, you're 4 you're, your 5 you're, you're, your

Vocabulary

1 cat 2 replace 3 commence 4 cousin 5 stroll 6 climb 7 hotel 8 rose 9 heat 10 holly

Page 31 Verbs

A 1 offered, lend 2 ran, finished 3 called, went 4 comes, whistle 5 Run, play, suggested 6 ate, dug, cut, trimmed 7 come, read, said 8 tossed, struck, sank 9 rode, fell, cut 10 swerved, scored
B 1 weep 2 cure 3 walk 4 touch 5 rise 6 quack 7 kick 8 wade 9 twirl 10 listen 11 rotate 12 obey 13 mend 14 grasp 15 finish 16 undo 17 subtract 18 purchase 19 nibble 20 surrender

Page 32 Adjectives

A 1 downcast, muddy, first
2 two, considerate, elderly, busy
3 continuous, holiday, dismal
4 four, experienced, sheer, slippery
5 impressive, three, triumphant, American, successful, vast
6 heavy, grey, torrential, exciting
B 1 agonizing 2 wicked 3 incomparable 4 colossal 5 gorgeous
C 1 – 15 Check you child's answers.

Page 33 Spelling

disappear, chocolate, secondary, address, calendar, temperature, detach, cupboard, miniature, parliament, miscellaneous, marvellous

Comparing adjectives

1 tall, **taller, tallest** 2 safe, **safer, safest** 3 heavy, **heavier, heaviest** 4 noisy, **noisier, noisiest** 5 honest, **more honest, most honest** 6 intelligent, **more intelligent, most intelligent** 7 good, **better, best** 8 old, **older, oldest** 9 bad, **worse, worst** 10 thoughtful, **more thoughtful, most thoughtful**

Vocabulary

A 1 enter 2 ascend 3 retreat 4 descend
5 crawl 6 advance 7 leave 8 follow
B 1 – 6 Check your child's answers.

Page 34 – 35 Comprehension

1a Salonica b south
2 Yes (Check your child's answer for the reasons to support this.)
3 He is terrified; the last voice he heard was of a guard.
4 He wasn't used to voices.
5 They sat down to smoke a cigarette.
6 Their speech was very different to the man that David was used to.
7 David thought he had seen the car before at the camp
8 The sound of the car caused David to 'stiffen'.
9 "David's feet were no longer part of him", "…his feet followed their own path independently…" and "his feet carried him over the bridge".
10 Check your child's answer and the reasons to support this.
11 Check your child's title is suitable for the extract.
12 Check that your child has understood the meaning of the phrases.
13 Check your child's sentences.
14 Check you child's answers e.g. a adverbs – independently, noiselessly, confidently b prepositions – over, up, of c common nouns – feet, bridge, teeth d pronouns – him, he, it e verbs – cared, avoided, whispered f adjecties – over and over, different, difficult

Page 36 Verbs

1 – 8 Check your child's verbs are suitable.

Rhyming words

1 height 2 same 3 bough 4 streak 5 pier
6 hearth 7 maim 8 frown

Homonyms

1 steal 2 meat 3 write 4 hoes 5 buoy
6 waist 7 bare 8 read 9 tail 10 mist
11 fowl 12 gilt

Page 37 Prepositions

1 with 2 to, about 3 over 4 beside 5 for
6 among 7 in 8 from 9 between
10 through

Joining sentences

1 We stayed at the hotel which overlooks the bay.
2 A man fell into the river while we were swimming.
3 Will you have lemonade or do you prefer shandy?
4 This story is very strange but it really happened.
5 The wind and rain stopped the cricket match so we decided to go home.

Of or off

1 I saw the old man fall off the bus.
2 One of my friends caught a large pike.
3 As soon as the plane took off several of us felt ill.
4 Two of Mr. Aitken's cows ran off down the road.
5 Of course you will be goalkeeper unless the game is off.

Synonyms

1 uneven 2 hide 3 right 4 forbid 5 copy
6 courage 7 void 8 round 9 begin 10 weak
11 defend 12 help

Page 38 Prepositions

1 The reward was shared equally **among** Paul, Simon and Andrew.
2 Sally was eating her lunch all **by** herself.
3 The watchman came **off** duty at 7.00 am.
4 Eight comes **after** seven and nine.
5 Terry ran **through** the winning post in record time.
6 Do you live **in** a town or a village?
7 A rabbit is different in several ways **from** a hare.
8 Heather rested her elbows **on** the desk.
9 The food was shared equally **between** the two dogs.
10 Patrick may not be **at** school this afternoon.
11 Pour the water **into** the bowl.
12 Mary hasn't received any letters **from** her friends.

Analogies

1 feminine 2 king 3 son 4 Mr 5 woman
6 niece 7 waiter 8 him 9 duchess 10 bride
11 wizard 12 widower

Page 39 there or their

1 their 2 There 3 there, their 4 their
5 There, their 6 there, their

Adverbs from nouns
1 Pat played the piano **skilfully**.
2 The climbers proceeded **cautiously** across the glacier.
3 The doctor cared **devoutly** for his patients.
4 Stephanie answered the questions **sensibly**.
5 Our school **generously** supported the earthquake disaster appeal.

Completing sentences
1 his 2 has, it 3 has, its 4 it 5 has

Opposites
1 early 2 down 3 same 4 exit 5 enemy
6 never 7 to 8 failure 9 in 10 over 11 long
12 shallow

Page 40 Direct speech
1 "Help!" she screamed. "The boat is sinking."
2 "Please open the window," Mr. Allinson said. "I find it stuffy."
3 "If you call me mean once more," warned Malcolm, "I'll hit you."
4 "Excuse me, Mrs. Thomas," said Peter, "but I think you have left your umbrella."
5 In a quiet voice Lucy asked, "May I have my ball back?"
6 "Stay where you are!" The farmer shouted to us.
7 "I am very grateful for the invitation," said Michael, "but I am afraid I shan't be able to accept."
8 His mother told him, "You must be back by nine o'clock."
9 "Have you seen my dog?" the old man inquired. "It ran off early this morning."
10 "Yes, I did eat all the cake," admitted Andrew, "but I was very hungry."

Spelling
1 piece 2 also 3 receive 4 quantity
5 invisible 6 government 7 excitement
8 visitor 9 library 10 altogether
11 different 12 development

Opposites – prefixes
1 insincere 2 imperfect 3 unlawful
4 nonsense 5 impossible 6 disorder
7 untruthful 8 disallow 9 unwelcome
10 dishonour 11 irresponsible
12 incomplete
Check your child's sentences.

Page 41 Sayings
1 to run off 2 bored/have nothing to do
3 irresponsible or worthless person 4 a flaw that detracts from enjoyment 5 very rarely 6 make up 7 very anxious 8 start afresh 9 ruin 10 able to achieve something

Completing sentences
1 – 10 Check that your child's answers are suitable.

Spelling
1 visible 2 sensible 3 responsible
4 terrible 5 portable

Page 42 Picture vocabulary
1 ballet shoes – a ballet dancer
2 flippers – a sea diver
3 skis – a skier
4 waders – a fisherman
5 spikes – a track runner
6 hiking boots – a walker/hiker
7 clown boots – a clown
8 snow shoes – an Eskimo
9 ice skates – an ice-skater
10 cowboy boots – a cowboy

Noun groups
Parts of the body ankle, arm, skull, neck, wrist
Animals wasp, badger, bat, falcon, snail
Buildings bank, factory, tower, hotel, school
rounders, scoop, bark, net

Sayings
1 to either succeed or fail 2 secrets will escape 3 tired/exhausted 4 can't cope with a situation 5 not to take sides in an argument 6 with every good thing that happens there is always a bad thing and this needs to be accepted 7 don't hold grudges 8 an achievement 9 to brag and self congratulate 10 don't bring up old grudges or past disagreements

Page 43 Punctuation
1 "Here's Philip. Let's ask him to come with us." said Bruce.
2 "Does Mr. Rigby still mend clocks?" inquired Elaine.
3 "You're not always right, you know," said Adrian.
4 Denise shouted to her mother, "Will you answer the telephone!"
5 Robert looked at the muddy field and said, "I'll be surprised if we start the match."

6 "Keep on practising Marilyn," urged her piano teacher, "you will master this difficult piece."

7 "Where does Britain obtain most of its rubber?" asked Fred.

8 "Is the Soviet Union one country," asked Hilary, "or is it a number of countries together?"

9 "The Pacific," said Mr. Brady, "is the largest of the world's oceans."

10 "Stop!" shouted the policeman, "you can't go down Market Street because there's a burst water main."

Homonyms

A 1 bridle **2** berth **3** serial **4** profit **5** waste **6** scene **7** muscle **8** colonel **9** pause **10** wood **11** draught **12** vein **13** soared **14** principal **15** check

B Check your child's answers.

Page 44 Whose or who's

1 who's **2** Who's **3** whose **4** whose **5** who's **6** Whose **7** who's **8** whose

Prepositions

1 at **2** with **3** on **4** with **5** from **6** to **7** in **8** for

Vocabulary

1 – 6 Check you child's answers.

Page 45 Collective nouns

1 swarm **2** aircraft **3** library **4** animals **5** magistrates **6** army **7** nest **8** chickens **9** anthology

Spanish city: Salamanca

Proverbs

swallow, eggs, inch, distance, honesty, turn

English river: Thames

Opposites

1 maximum **2** bent **3** temporary **4** ugly **5** false **6** yes **7** foolish **8** solid **9** defeat **10** junior **11** transparent **12** fertile

Secret message: last exercise

Page 46 – 47 Comprehension

1 russet and black

2 lists, galleries, banks of turf, branches of trees, the steeple of a church and the royal gallery

3 Men-at-arms would keep order at the entrances.

4 A farrier is a person who shoes horses.

5 An armourer makes and mends armour.

6 The duties of the heralds was to open the wooden gates.

7 They were situated there because it offered a less shocking view of the combat.

8 The blood and gore of the fight.

9 Those of a better degree than the vulgar observers.

10 Because people had to climb trees and watch from the church steeple therefore it must be overcrowded.

11 palisades – a strong fence made of stakes driven into the ground

pennons – a long flag

gallery – an upper level of seating

canopy – a roofed structure serving as shelter

12a afforded **b** beyond **c** adorned **d** temporary **e** terminated **f** verge

13 Check your child's answer.

14 Check your child's drawing.

15 Check that your child's title is suitable for the extract.

Page 48 Verbs

1 – 12 Check your child's use of verbs.

Possession

1 a men's hairdressers **2** the artist's paints **3** a children's library **4** the babies' toys **5** a pensioners' concert **6** a pets' corner **7** the singer's voice **8** the girls' tennis rackets **9** James's cricket bat **10** the geese's feathers

Silent letters

1 dumb **2** island **3** salmon **4** listen **5** gnome **6** wrong **7** bomber **8** knuckle **9** palm **10** leopard **11** drawer **12** solemn

Nouns from verbs

1 arrival **2** punishment **3** movement **4** complaint **5** departure **6** donation **7** memory **8** destruction **9** imagination **10** enlargement **11** captive **12** applause **13** belief **14** alteration **15** conclusion